NATURAL WEATHER WISDOM

by
Uncle Offa

"I tell you it's March!"

"One day telleth another, and one night certifieth another."

Psalm XIX Verse 2

D1425235

Script by Frederick Hingston
Illustrated by Leonard C. Gilley

Published in 1991 by
The Self Publishing Association Ltd
Units 7/10 Hanley Workshops
Hanley Swan, Worcs
A MEMBER OF

in association with
FREDERICK HINGSTON

British Library Cataloguing in Publication Data

A catalogue record for this book is
available from the British Library

ISBN   1 85421 151 X (Paperback)
        1 85421 146 3 (Hardback)

Designed & produced by Images Design & Print Ltd, Hanley Swan
Printed & bound in Great Britain by Billing & Sons, Worcester

Contents

To Fred
who kept my identity secret

It's you or me!

The Salt Seller
Medicine for the cold, the wind, etc
. . . To be taken with a pinch of salt

Foreword

Why is it that on my way to Dorset for a long and lazy weekend, ten seconds after the weather forecast has finished on the car radio the only bit I remember is that it's raining in the Isle of Skye, or snowing in the outer Hebrides? Similarly, on my way to East Anglia to view the waving fields of golden corn it's likely the weather forecast for Dyfed and Pembroke will be the one that lodges in my irrational mind.

And yet is my mind the only one that's irrational? I doubt it. I know several people, including close relatives, who make a point of watching, or listening or reading weather forecasts because "it helps me plan my day", and yet when I ask them if it's going to rain this afternoon, they simply haven't a clue.

What is the attraction of the weather? As I write this, my colleagues and I make the daily early morning farming programmes on BBC Radio 4 . . . a daily mixture of politics, finance and science, all of it crucial, you'd have thought, for a successful farm business. But on several occasions, trying to find out what my customers think of my programmes, they reply . . . "oh yes, the farming programmes. Love the weather forecast. Best one on the radio." To which I reply, "What about the price trends, or the latest political developments in

Brussels, which have taken me all night to prepare and which have used up enormous amounts of editorial judgement . . ."

Which makes it quite obvious why, after years of trying to please a rural and agricultural audience with top level political nuances and the most sophisticated price trends this side of the City, I was so pleased when Uncle Offa hove into view.

Well, that should have been my reaction. After all, I claim to know what my audience wants. In fact I said something like "more bloody weather aaarrgh!" But after one of my colleagues got me down off the ceiling and gave me a cup of black coffee, I began to see the possibilities. Let's get rid of the real weather forecast once a month and just let Uncle Offa have a go. If they're all so keen on the weather, I thought, instead of giving them a forecast, why not just give them a few rhymes and old sayings, throw in a few dates and let them work it out for themselves.

Without much of a trumpet fanfare, Uncle Offa was launched on an unsuspecting Radio 4 audience on the last Saturday of September 1990. At 6.46 am. Well, you'd have thought we were giving away free tickets to the Farmers Club Ball. Not all the sixty or seventy callers correctly identified the Radio 4 farming office as the source of such expressions as "If ducks do swim at Hallowtide, at Christmas these same ducks will slide." But just to make sure they were going to get their calls and letters answered, a fair proportion wrote directly to the BBC chairman and director general. No, they didn't know what this Uncle Offa was either, but they sure as hell were going to find out, if only to reduce their mail to sensible proportions once more.

And so Uncle Offa became a small institution, a monthly treat for the quarter of a million or so people who are driving their cars, their combines, their sheep, their taxis and their tractors long before the rest of the world has got up. Uncle Offa himself now quietly admits to having a fully-paid up fan club, which includes my mother. I wonder if she was one of those relatives I mentioned at the beginning . . .?

All I want to know, and I'm sorry to have to spoil the party in this way . . . has anybody ever made an accurate note of one month's weather and then looked back at the predictions included in one of Uncle Offa's texts? And if so, was Uncle Offa even close to being correct?

I asked this question once on the radio, and the silence was deafening. Perhaps the weather itself doesn't matter after all, it's just fun being able to talk about it.

Tim Finney

Tim Finney
BBC Radio Agriculture Editor
MAY 1991

Introduction

Undoubtedly the most popular subject of conversation amongst the British must be the weather. When two people meet they exchange greetings, then turn automatically to the weather. Concern is expressed if it looks uncertain and anxious questions are asked. But the answers given are usually based on wild speculation and are seldom accurate or reliable. How nice it would be if one could speak with authority!

The purpose of this book therefore is to explain how to foretell the weather in your area as correctly as possible. The methods expounded are ancient, their origins lost in the mists of time, but it is certain they date from before the Roman Conquest. Since that time they have received additions from generations of observant countrymen and there is now a mass of information available in the form of sayings, beliefs, old saws, poems, rhymes and jingles, all purporting to reveal what the weather has in store for us. Collected together, they add up to a very rich treasury of wisdom.

I have always been interested in the way in which true countrymen seem able to foretell the weather, and so, about thirty five years ago, I determined to unravel the mystery of their skill: I started to keep a record of country weather saws in a notebook. It took me a long time to gather sufficient facts and beliefs to be able to discern any pattern behind the wealth of random data, but eventually a pattern did emerge, with certain dominant signs forming the basis or framework of the forecasting system. Once I had observed and noted these signs, I found that the weather habitually kept more or less within the framework formed by them, and was unlikely ever to stray outside it for long. A multitude of other signs filled in the foreground of the weather pattern, the whole adding up to a comprehensive and astonishingly accurate picture of the weather to come.

It was when I moved to my present address in Wales that I decided to make my accumulated knowledge public. I started out in the parish magazine and later in the local newspaper. A grave snag quickly arose. I was a newcomer, itself an offence. Furthermore, I was not even a Welshman, which compounded the offence. A nom-de-plume was demanded, and I adopted that of Uncle Offa, my village being within a Sabbath Day's journey of Offa's Dyke. Nearly everybody in the area has now heard of Uncle Offa; and at least twenty different people have been identified as the weather prophet. But very few of them have got it right. The mystery of anonymity appears to have lent credence to my prognostications: the words of Uncle Offa are respected by many who would pay them scant regard if they knew who he really is. Indeed, my personal predictions are usually greeted with scorn.

We have, of course, the Meteorological Office, the weather satellites and a host of other modern, sophisticated and efficient sources of information, and very good they are, too. It may therefore be asked why we should bother trying to tell our own weather. The answer is simple: the most you can expect from the national broadcasts will be something referring to "South-West England, Wales, and West Midlands", followed by some three sentences to cover the whole area; this is usually accurate as far as it goes, but it does not go far enough to tell you if it will rain in your garden tomorrow, and *that* is what matters to you. For this same reason, you should note that the general weather pattern in the north of the country is very different from that in the south, and some of the sayings in this book apply only in limited areas. It is best to use common sense, to note the track records of each and to follow those which have the best ones in your area. Generally, the sayings quoted in this book are applicable all over the country: particular local ones have been avoided.

So there is still a place, and a necessary place, for the soothsayer, well-grounded in the lore and wisdom of our forefathers, who alone can foretell the local conditions with accuracy. This book sets out to tell you how to go about this, in the hope that you will be able to achieve a higher degree of accuracy, to the great benefit of yourself, your friends and neighbours.

I am often asked why these old sayings should be true, as many of them appear absurd or fantastic. I am forced to reply simply that I cannot tell you. But it should be remembered that the vast majority of them have stood the test of time, while being tested and used by men to whom an accurate forecast was vital. I myself have made use of most of them over the years, and in several cases my personal opinion as to their dependability appears in the text. But I cannot answer the question WHY? As an example, I firmly believe in the Days of Prediction. These emerged from history as established holy days, and were sanctified by having Christian saints appointed to them. But I cannot suggest any reason why they should have such a remarkable capacity for foretelling the weather. Another example is the chaffinch who lives close to my study window, and calls "Weet-weet, weet-weet," just before it rains. He always does it and he has never given a false alarm. But I cannot tell you why. So, since my object is to tell you how to forecast the weather, I must ask you simply to accept this mass of ancient lore as fact. If you don't believe it, try some of it out yourself.

I have managed to assemble a large number of primitive beliefs, old saws, rhymes, jingles and assertions, and it may be that the sheer bulk of them will over-awe the reader. If this should be the case, please turn to Chapter Nine, which explains how they all fit together. But as a start, I would recommend that you make careful notes of the weather on the Days of Prediction and at the turns of the moon. If you read these correctly, you will be more than halfway to becoming a sound weather forecaster. Thereafter, add as much or as little of the remaining data as you feel inclined. It is inevitable that in a book of this nature, there will be some overlap and cross-referencing; for this I apologise and hope that the categories I have used will make for something between easy reading and quick checking.

If after reading through this book, you still feel that the whole thing is a pile of rubbish, I would draw your attention to a quote that I have printed on the title page. It is taken from the Book of Psalms, Number 19, Verse 2. "One day telleth another and one night certifieth another." Or, as it is given in the Revised Version, "Day unto day uttereth speech, and night unto night sheweth knowledge."

The entries in this book have come from a myriad of different sources, including farmers, keepers, poachers, naturalists and all sorts of countrymen, as well as books, newspapers, periodicals, radio and television. By no means least are the many and valuable contributions which have come from the stalwart body of pen friends who have written to me as a result of my monthly broadcasts on Radio Four's *Farming Week*. They have supplied me with many sayings which were new to me; they have introduced me to books that I did not know, and one of them even introduced me to my publisher, an invaluable service. I cannot thank them enough. Their help and advice have been priceless. It is not possible for me to thank everyone who has contributed to my store of knowledge individually. But that does not lessen my gratitude to them for their help. I must, however, mention two for their particular contributions. The first is the staff of the Meteorological Office for permission to make use of their "quiet" and "stormy" periods, of which more anon. The second is Peterborough of the *Daily Telegraph*, for the gem with which I now conclude.

Under the dateline 19th October 1987, just after the great hurricane –

> "Our beleaguered weather forecasters might be interested to know that weather forecasting in China's south-west province of Hunan is done by children. The pupils, whose predictions are reputed to be extremely accurate, observe the local weather patterns and any unusual behaviour by animals. They then correlate these with weather maxims before issuing their predictions by loudspeaker."

This is the wisdom of the Orient, indeed. But if they can do it, so can we.

F.B.H.
1991.

Weather forecasting is done in China's S.W Province of Hunan by Children

Chapter One

The Days of Prediction

The science of reading the weather signs and forecasting the weather has been a principal concern of mankind since he first walked this earth. It will so continue until his time has ended. Man has always had to struggle for his survival against the vagaries of the weather. A bad season could wipe out his crops or his flocks and leave him starving, so it has always been a matter of life and death to him that he should be able to foretell the weather as correctly as possible. It has been even harder for the Englishman, for he alone has had to cope with the exceptional moods of the English weather. Those who survived were those who got it right; and it was they who built up a weather lore to pass on to their successors. The origins of this lore are time out of mind. The earliest and most primitive religions throughout the world were bound up with an ability to forecast or control the weather. Good weather prophets became great men in their communities, credited with mystical powers and held in deep respect. Men knew that the sun brought warmth and life to the world: its courses, its solstices and its equinoxes were carefully noted, and the rhythm of the year was faithfully recorded. It is certain that our Neolithic forebears studied and understood a great deal about it, and the first calendars, the stone circles, came into being.

'I tell you it's March!'

But a simple marking of the seasons was a long way from predicting the English weather. Even today, with weather stations and satellites all round us, our experts sometimes get it wrong, and one could be forgiven for thinking that our highly variable weather defies exact prediction. Nevertheless, Bronze Age Man had to get it right or die, so weather forecasting was of necessity the principal study of the priests and the intelligentsia of those days.

Somewhere back in the mists of time a peculiarity was detected in the calendar. It was found that the weather on certain days of the year tended to set a pattern for the following few weeks. They became important, red letter days. They had so much influence on men's lives, they became occasions for intercession to the sun or to the spirit of the day, holy days on which to plead for good weather for the crops and herds. They are called the Days of Prediction.

The Days were certainly known to the Druids and they are discernible in their stone circles. Later, during the 450 years of the Roman occupation from 55BC to 412AD, they were acknowledged and respected by these foreign invaders and formed part of their own philosophy of life. It was during the Roman occupation of our islands that Christianity reached us, and the Christian priests, also acknowledging their importance, gave the Days their blessing by allocating a saint to each one. People often ask how the commemoration of a saint on a certain date somehow lends that day powers of prophecy. Briefly, it doesn't. It is because the date has been known for aeons to be a Day of Prediction that the saint was afterwards hitched on to it.

Do these days really prophesy the weather? Let it be recorded right from the start that nothing in weather forecasting is infallible, NOTHING. But the Days of Prediction have stood the test of time. They give a very strong indication of the weather to come, and if all the signs are correctly noted

24

and balanced, one against another, a surprising accuracy can be achieved, something around eighty-five per cent.

The weather signs can indeed tell us a great deal about the future. Watch a farmer when he emerges from his house of a morning. His first act is to glance up at the sky. He is reading the weather signs to foretell what the day has in store for him. He knows that the signs are there in the sky, in the ground and in the wind, in the behaviour of the animals and birds, in the trees and the plants, indeed in everything around him. The signs are there, all he has to do is read them.

But first, a word of warning. Forecasting by weather signs is a very local business and the signs are unlikely to give a true reading beyond the confines of the parish. It is obvious that because seagulls act in a certain way at Land's End, it tells one nothing about the weather at John O'Groats. Similarly, a shower of rain in Kent has no effect on Edinburgh. The man who can extend his predictions to cover a whole county, with fifty per cent accuracy, is a genius. The man who spouts confident predictions to cover the whole country for the whole year ahead, is a fool. There may indeed be people who have a wisdom which enables them to foretell what will happen over a wide area for some time ahead. But if they were *consistently* accurate, everybody, including the Ministry of Agriculture, the NFU and the RAF, would hang on their words, treating them with the respect due to royalty. They would be famous, nationally-known figures. But there are no such figures, because reading the weather signs gives only local results.

'Natural' forecasting is very local . . . it only extends as far as your parish

How far ahead can the weather be predicted? One of the Days of Prediction, St Paul's Day, is said to reveal the weather for the whole year ahead. I maintain that is is a good guide for perhaps the next six months, but has a tendency to tail off after that. There are some, of which St Swithin is by the far the best-known, which prognosticate the next thirty or forty days. The moon, too, is a fair guide for up to twenty-eight days, and there are various signs which give a good indication of the weather for the whole summer. But the vast majority of signs do not look more than twenty-four hours ahead. So, true prediction is a combination of the long, the fairly long and the immediate.

The Days of Prediction are as follows:

25th January	St Paul's Day
2nd February	Candlemas Day
21st March	St Benedict
Good Friday	
25th May	St Urban
15th June	St Vitus
24th June	St John
15th July	St Swithin
6th August	Transfiguration
24th August	St Bartholomew
29th September	St Michael (Michaelmas)
11th November	St Martin (Martinmas)
21st December	St Thomas

St Paul's Day 25th January

When foretelling the weather on this day, it is necessary to observe and note down its phases hour by hour, or even half hourly, throughout the day from six a.m. to six p.m. This is due to the belief that the hours of the day will reflect the weather month by month throughout the year. The belief certainly holds some truth; I have known years when a prediction was about ninety per cent correct, and even one year which was one hundred per cent correct. Generally, the signs are dependable up to the end of July, but not so much so thereafter.

An old jingle runs –

"If Paul's Day be fair and clear
We shall have a happy year.
But if we have but wind and rain
Dear will be all sorts of grain.
If clouds and mist do mark the sky
Great store of birds and beasts will die."

Another old prophecy, which I first heard in Devon, runs as follows –

"If St Paul's Day be fine expect a good harvest.
If it is wet or snowy expect a famine.
If it is windy expect a war."

– The prophecies contained in the first two lines appear to be singularly correct. I have not checked on the third!

Auntie Dyke

Candlemas Day 2nd February

Occurring at about the worst time of the year, when people are thinking longingly about the heat of summer (which probably has some influence on their thinking), this day is supported by a host of sayings.

> "If Candlemas Day be clear and bright
> Winter will have another flight.
> But if it be dark with clouds and rain
> Winter is gone and will not come again."

> "Cold weather on Candlemas means colder weather after
> the feast than before." (translated from the Latin)

> "If Candlemas Day be bright and clear
> Half the winter's to come this year.
> If Candlemas Day be cloudy and black
> It bears the winter away on its back." (Wiltshire)

> "If the sun be bright on Candlemas, there will be more
> frost after the feast than before." (Nottinghamshire)

All these sayings carry the same message: that a dull Candlemas Day indicates the end of the winter. One final saying –

> "Wherever the wind is on Candlemas Day
> There it will stay to the end of May."

Candlemas incidentally is the first of the Wind Forecasts days which are worth noting, for they tend to be very reliable. This particular one, however, is out of tune with the other four, because the others are the quarter days and each has a span of ninety days. I would advise that you treat it with more caution than the others.

St Benedict's Day 21st March

> "As the wind is on St Benedict's Day, so it will stay
> for three months."

This rather bold and emphatic statement may sometimes appear to contradict St Paul's forecast, but rest assured that St

Paul declares the weather only in general terms, and says nothing about the specific wind direction. Following after St Benedict, the next day to foretell the wind is 24th June, St John's Day, which is just ninety-five days later. The four main days which are associated with the wind direction are amongst the most reliable in the calendar. But bear in mind that they speak of *prevailing* winds; there will probably be periodical deviations. Be guided by St Benedict rather than Candlemas, if Candlemas and St Benedict's Day should prove mutually contradictory.

Palm Sunday and *Good Friday*

It may well be asked how our Neolithic forebears managed to make predictions about Palm Sunday and Good Friday, bearing in mind that they are both Christian and moveable feasts. The answer is to be found in the name Easter, which derives from Eastre, the Saxon Moon-Goddess, whose festival was celebrated at this time of year. Following the Lunar Year, March 21st, the equinox, was then New Year's Day and the festival was celebrated at the first full moon thereafter. When the early Church was being established it took over the festival for its own celebrations, and so Easter came into being as the first weekend after that full moon. The Day of Prediction may have been the full moon in past times, but today it is regarded as Good Friday.

31

Easter is a movable feast

The saws for Palm Sunday and Good Friday are as follows –

"If on Palm Sunday there be rain, that be tokeneth to goodness.
If it thunder on that day, then it signifieth a merrie year."

Palm Sunday is a fairly reliable prediction date, but Good Friday has an even better track record. An old jingle runs –

"Rain on Good Friday and Easter Day,
A good year for grass and a bad year for hay."

– in other words, a wet year. My own personal observation, which I maintain is most reliable, declares that the weather on Good Friday will be maintained for forty days thereafter. Here's another – "Rainy Easter, a cheese year." – This is one saying for which the logic is quite simple: grass needs rain, good grass gives good milk yields, hence a wet year gives a good cheese year.

St Urban 25th May

Our forebears asserted, simply and bluntly – "St Urban gives the Summer" – and many people would agree. It is certain that the day will give at least a fair indication of what the weather will be like, but be warned: the signs can often be ambiguous or a little optimistic.

St Vitus 15th June

> "If St Vitus Day be rainy weather
> T'will rain for forty days together."

As it stands this can prove a very gloomy forecast because St Swithin's Day – the best-known rain date of them all – is only thirty days ahead, the implication being seventy days of rain! I firmly believe that the original jingle said *thirty* days, not forty, which would cover the period in between the two days. If this belief is accepted, the rule will be found to be a more reliable one. There is only the one jingle about St Vitus, but the rhymes about rain dates are fewer than those which concern the wind.

St John's Day 24th June (Midsummer Day/ Quarter Day)

> "As the wind is on St John's Day so it will be for three months."

> "Midsummer (Day) rain spoils hay and grain."

There are many more sayings relating to this day, which will be given later in their appropriate contexts. It is clearly a very important one: as well as being the longest day, it is the Summer Solstice, the day when the sun rises and sets at its most northerly points. In the Druidical religion and in Witchery (Witchcraft) the most important ceremonies of the year were held to mark it.

St Swithin 15th July

Those who find the authenticity of the Days of Prediction hard to believe should reflect on St Swithin. Most people in the country are familiar with the significance of this day, and most of them – probably more than half – believe it. It may be the only Day of Prediction known to the public at large, the last surviving shred of a primitive understanding, but the others are no less significant and no less reliable – all of them have their place in the pattern of forecasting.

"St Swithin's Day if thou dost rain,
Full forty days it will remain.
St Swithin's Day, if thou art fair
Full forty days 't'will rain nae mair."

'It would rain today!'

Or, as Shakespeare puts it –

> "If on St Swithin's feast the welkin lours,
> And every pent house streams with hasty showers
> Twice twenty days shall clouds their fleeces drain
> And wash the pavements with incessant rain."

– Powerful stuff! but the message is the same in each version. In actual fact, St Swithin's Day is usually a "bit-of-both" day: half wet and half sunny. As the Met Office say, "sunny intervals and showers". Nature, I believe, does like to make our job more difficult! So, my advice to the novice weather forecaster is to adopt an enigmatic stance under these circumstances, particularly when the "Swithin Only" faction are holding forth. Try: "You mark my words. St Swithin's message is not so straightforward as all that." Follow it with a shake of the head. Nobody will understand you, but you will be covered, whichever way the cat may jump, and your reputation will be assured.

Transfiguration 6th August

> "As the weather is on the Day of the Transfiguration so
> it will be for the rest of the year."

I first heard this gem in Dorset and later in Devon, but I am not one of its more enthusiastic advocates. It is over-ambitious, unreliable and out of rhythm with the other Days of Prediction, which occur at regular intervals throughout the year. Probably the saying is of far more recent origin, perhaps thought up by some religious fanatic, or by someone who wanted to enhance the importance of the day. The saying has certainly caught on, but it is, in my opinion, *not* one of the original Days; as such, extreme caution is advisable in its application.

St Bartholomew 24th August

St Bartholomew is quite straightforward –

> "All the tears that St Swithin can cry
> St Bartelmy's mantle will wipe dry."

Note that the word here is "will", not "may". If St Swithin is wet, then St Bartholomew will dry it up (be warned, however, that this forecast is sometimes out by as much as three days either way). But if St Swithin is dry, the following applies –

> "If Bartholomew's be fine and clear
> Then hope for a prosperous Autumn that year."

Note also that this saw speaks of fine weather and says nothing about rain. After this day you should expect dull or fine weather, but not, as a rule, much rain. There are, of course, exceptional years, but then there are exceptions to every rule and precept in weather forecasting, as in everything else.

St Michael 29th September (Quarter Day)

> "As the wind is on St Michael's Day so 't'will be for three months."

This latter saying is another fairly dependable indication as to the direction of the wind. The trouble is that it occurs around the period of the equinoxial gales, which may give a false reading locally. If the gales coincide with the saint's day, watch the wind direction for two days after they have subsided. This way you will get a truer reading and forecast.

October incidentally has more weather signs than any other month, but it has no Day of Prediction.

St Michael – Quarter Day, and therefore a windy day

Oh! St Michael!

Martinmas 11th November

The weather on St Martin's Day is said to foretell the weather for three months; furthermore, where the wind blows on Martinmas Eve, "there 't'will remain for the rest of the winter". This prediction is reinforced with the awful threat – "Wind North-West on Martinmas and a severe Winter to come." It all sounds a bit gloomy, but what can one expect at this time of year? October and November are both crammed with weather signs concerning the oncoming winter and specific months in the New Year. For instance, St Clement's Day 23rd November, is said to give the weather for February. Give heed to these sayings, for they often add up to a very accurate picture.

St Thomas' Day 21st December

> "Look at the weathercock on St Thomas' Day, the wind
> will remain there for three months."

There are those who maintain that "St Thomas' Day" should actually read "Christmas Day", but St Thomas's does have a better track record. There are a string of other sayings pertaining to Christmas Day, but most of them would hold up better if they were associated with the Solstice, which is, of course, St Thomas Day. All these are given in the next chapters.

39

* * * * * *

The Days of Prediction form the foundation of all weather forecasting in this country. The monthly signs are built onto them, and the combination gives a fair outline of the weather to come. The many hundreds of other signs form the cladding to complete the structure. The individual who bases his predictions on one sign alone, as many do on St Swithin, is most unlikely to make an accurate forecast. It is a matter of collecting all the evidence, sifting and assessing it and awarding the various signs their due significance. If this is done conscientiously and correctly, you can achieve a high degree of accuracy.

Chapter Two

The Moon

Next in importance to the Days of Prediction are the phases and influences of the moon, which has a more profound effect on our lives than most of us realise. We all know that this great hunk of matter, circling the World only a quarter of a million miles away, draws the waters of the earth towards it, causing the tides to ebb and flow. In the same way, though less predictably, the moon affects the atmospheric pressure, altering the weather as it does so. The period of the full moon certainly has an effect on many animals, as well as human beings. In days gone by, the insane were referred to as "lunatics" because, it was contended, their condition worsened as the moon came to the full and improved as it waned. Other stories told of people losing their wits if they slept out of doors habitually under a full moon. I was assured once that having one's hair cut during the period of the waxing moon, would delay baldness longer than if it was cut during the waning period! How on earth would you prove something like this? The idea conjures up intriguing visions of men having only one side of their hair cut in alternate phases of the moon!

"I know I pull the tides but this is ridiculous!"

The powers attributed to the moon are legion, and its influence on the weather is borne witness by the great number of sayings associated with it. For example, "The weather at the turn of the moon" – i.e. at the full or new moon – "foretells the weather until the next turn." – This is a general principle, but there are those who argue the weather change comes just before, or soon after the change of the moon.

From the *New Book of Knowledge*, published 1758, we learn – "Do not predict from the first night of a new moon but from a couple of nights later." A saying from Surrey states that – "If, after an indifferent new moon, the third day is fine, the weather will change for the better in its second quarter." According to Pliny – "the prime, or fourth day after the change of the moon do most commonly determine the force and direction of the wind." Sir Francis Bacon would have it that – "From long observation sailors suspect storms on the fifth day of the moon." And a Spanish saying runs – "If the weather on the sixth day after the new moon is the same as on the fourth day, the same weather will continue for the whole moon."

Official and Informed Opinion, when asked to give a ruling as to the validity of these sayings, brushed them aside with the one word "Poppycock", so we turned instead to Experience: she showed that there is a great deal of truth in them, despite their apparent variations. Age may not bring wisdom but experience certainly breeds sagacity.

Here is a range of local sayings –

"If it rains at the new moon, there will be rain every day until the next new moon." (Derbyshire).

"When the moon turns over" – i.e. new or full – "you see the weather for the next fortnight." (Wiltshire)

"The Full moon brings good weather." (Gloucestershire – this is a rather bold one and should be treated with caution!)

I am not sure that any one of these sayings is fully reliable because the change in the weather does not always fall on the same day relative to the turn of the moon. Watch carefully in the early months of the year. It will be found that the change comes regularly on a certain day, i.e. one, two or three days before or after the change. When this day has been identified it will be found to remain consistently the same until the next Solstice.

There are many other sayings about the moon, some of which I have listed below –

"Clear Moon frost soon" – Obviously this is one which applies only during the winter months. It is quite reliable because, while clouds tend to blanket warmth in, a cloudless sky will naturally be colder and therefore more liable to frost.

"If the new moon lies on her back the weather will be dry, for she can hold water. If upright, she cannot do so and it will rain."
– Experience has taught me that this is a completely dependable weather sign.

"Sharp moon horns do threaten windy weather."

"Blunt horns, or an indistinct outline, forecast rain within twelve hours."

"In Winter and Spring, when the moon's horns are sharp and well defined, frost is to be expected."

Unfortunately none of these sayings leave much option for fine weather! Here are a few more which bode gloom and doom –

"It will be a wet month that has two full moons in it."
(A saying from Devon which I swear by.)

"If the new moon does not appear until the fourth day, it foretells a troubled time for the whole month."
(Derbyshire)

– The fourth day would appear to be a significant one, for an Essex saying runs – "When the moon first appears on the fourth day very clear and sharp and rather on the slant, it promises mostly fair weather for the month" – which is an example of similar features being given different interpretations in different parts of the country.

"Seeing you I thought it would rain"

"Saturday new and Sunday full, was never fine and always foul" – is one of those old sayings which refer to a specific and rare occurrence, and which are usually accurate – this one certainly is. From Devon again we have –

> "Pale moon means rain. Red moon means blow. White
> moon means neither but often means snow."

– The difficulty here lies in identifying the pale, red and white moons. It is not as easy as it might appear. Here is another – "In the decay of the moon a cloudy morning bodes a fair afternoon" – This one is certainly reliable, but it is also alleged that a misty morning bodes a fair afternoon at any stage of the moon, particularly in summer, and this too is dependable.

A pail moon – rain

47

Another particular moon-saying, this one from Nottingham, runs as follows – "A bright star near the new moon foretells windy weather." Also from Nottingham is the well-known and very dependable – "The first new moon of the year is stronger in its influence than the others." And from Lincoln we have – "A pale moon foretells wind and rain" – which is bound to be a valuable one, provided you can recognise a pale moon.

Just as a point of interest, it used to be said that pigs should be killed during the rise of the moon. If killed when the moon is waning, the fat of the pork would shrink. It seems almost incredible, but eighty to a hundred years ago, when every cottager kept a pig, all countrymen firmly believed in this.

I must mention here the phenomenon known as a ring around the moon. There are several sayings about this, all mutually contradictory. The differences arise because the various sayings originated in different parts of the country, where altitude, humidity and temperature affect the conditions. Due to this, it is not generally a reliable sign. Here are the various interpretations –

"Ring around the moon means rain."

"Halo around the moon means strong winds."
"A moon with a silver shield portends dry weather."

"Ring far, rain near, ring near, rain far."

My advice is that you should make your own observations and find the answers that are appropriate to your part of the world. Rely on them to the exclusion of all others.

Here is a rather nice one from Somerset, usually accurate –

"A general mist near the full moon before sunrise denotes fair weather for a fortnight. If this is seen in the new moon, there will be wet weather in the last fortnight of that moon."

In conclusion, here is a word of warning about a very common misconception. "Every schoolboy knows" that there are twelve calendar months in the year and thirteen lunar ones. But as every farmer will tell you, there are only twelve and a half lunar, or moon, months in a year. There are three hundred and sixty-five days in a calendar year, but only three hundred and fifty-four in twelve lunar months – were it not so, the turn of the moon would occur on the same day in every month, year after year. The fact that it is not so ensures that last year's weather is no guide to this year's. The balance of twelve days was once called the Holy Days, and these were inserted immediately after the Winter Solstice. Now they are referred to as the Twelve Days of Christmas, as in the well-known carol. So, beware of the false prophet who assures you that it is always fine (or wet or cold) on such and such a day. He is wrong – there is no such rule.

Unquestionably, the moon has a considerable influence on the weather. The reason why there are such apparent differences of opinion in what is written above is due to the fact that the moon's effects differ according to the part of the country in which the observation is made. With long and careful observation the moon can tell one a great deal about the weather to come. The results will fully reward the time and effort spent.

So let us end on a cheerful note, with this old adage from Rutland –

"When the clouds of the moon to the West fly away,
You may safely rely on a settled fair day."

Chapter Three

THE MONTHLY SIGNS - 1
The Long Term Forecasts

If the Days of Prediction form the skeleton of weather forecasting, and the first layers of flesh are added by the moon, then the sinews must be supplied by the monthly signs. These are generally not as reliable as the Days of Prediction but they are based on observations made by countrymen over the centuries and found to be habitually dependable. Some of the signs are ancient, dating back to Roman times, and some can only be traced back for two or three generations.

Because the weather signs were observed and recorded by countrymen for countrymen, they tend to refer to the effect of the weather on crops; after all, the whole of the agriculturalists' year is centred around the coming harvest. There are, for instance, no established sayings concerning the weather that we may expect for the Test Match at Lords! But an intelligent interpretation of the references to the crops can usually give a straight clue as to the weather. A poor forecast for wheat, for instance, indicates wet weather in July and

51

August, and a heavy apple crop points to a fine August and September. Similarly the hay crop is harvested at the end of May and in June, so any reference to a good hay crop implies fine weather then.

The months of October to January are often referred to as the period of the Long Term Weather Forecasts. February to May are the months which foretell the summer, and June to September are the Harvest Months, where the interest lies solely in tomorrow's weather.

October

October, the Golden Month, is the start of The Weather Prophet's year. The harvest is over, its yield is in the barn or the loft, the Harvest Thanksgiving Festival has been celebrated and the farmer starts to look forward, not without some concern, to next year's harvest. As a result, all the month's predictions look forward well into December and the New Year.

Of the month itself, one saying tells us that – "October has twenty-one fine days." This sounds a little over-optimistic, and some people prefer to say it is only nineteen; nevertheless, it is worth remembering that the month is usually more fine than rough.

Of St Luke's Day, 18th October, it is said – "St Luke's little summer is a fine day." – which is very true. St Luke usually gives four days to a week of lovely weather. But if one may be permitted to criticise a holy saint and gospel writer, let it be hinted that he is not always punctual. His summer has a tendency to arrive up to five days late! But rest assured, it will come. I have also heard it said that 28th October, the Feast of St Simon and St Jude, marks its end limit. The Met Office has noted the dates 16th to 29th as a quiet period, which upholds St Luke's declaration.

There are two December forecasts in the month. First – "Much rain in October, much wind in December." – Incidentally, the Germans have an identical saying. Second – "If ducks swim at Hallowtide, at Christmas these same ducks will slide." The Feast of Hallowe'en is, of course, 31st October. These two sayings are the only two that we have concerning the month of December.

There are many general winter predictions –

"For every October fog there will be snow in winter, heavy or light according to the fog."

"Full moon in October without frost, no frost till full moon in November."

– This saying is true up to a point: that point is reached in such places as high hills, frost pockets and the like, which may breach the rule. But for "normal" places the rule is golden.

Turning to the moon, we learn that –

53

"If the October moon is born with the points up, the month will be dry; if down, wet."

Then come the natural signs –

"If during leaf fall in October many leaves remain hanging, a frosty winter with much snow will follow."

"If in October the leaves still hold, the coming winter will be cold."

"Late leaf fall, hard New Year." – So pray for an early frost causing the early leaf fall.

"If the oak bears its leaves in October, there will be a hard winter." – This sign, specifying oak leaves, is usually the most reliable of this particular set.

Animals and birds can also tell us much about the oncoming winter. Look, for example, at a horse's coat: if the winter is to be a hard one, a horse instinctively grows its coat thick. Other sayings include –

"If foxes bark much in October they are calling up great falls of snow." – Even in the cities, the distinctive bark of the urban fox can usually be heard.

"If the hare wears a thick coat in October, he shows his wisdom. Lay in a good stock of fuel." – If you haven't any foxes or hares in your area, watch the sheep. If they cluster together and move slowly, it is a sure sign of snow.

"If squirrels early mass their hoard, expect a winter like a sword."

"When birds and badgers are fat in October, you may expect a cold winter."

"When owls hunt in daylight, expect a hard winter."

When Owls hunt in daylight in Autumn, there will be a hard Winter

"Tally ho, Fred?"

In the New Forest it is said that if the deer's coat is grey in October, the winter will be severe – I presume that the saying refers to the Red Deer.

In the bird world, if you see the greater spotted woodpecker hammering away at the sycamore tree, he is probably storing up insects against a cold spell.

Turning again to the trees and plants, we learn that an abundance of acorns, dead nettles and thick onion skins in October threaten a hard winter.

Here is one from America –

"When the chestnut leaves do fall, cotton ain't no good at all."

– My excuse for mentioning this one is that it is bound to be useful to British cotton growers!

All in all, there is plenty to warn us of what the winter will bring.

Moving on to January –

"If there is snow and frost in October, January will be mild."

"If October brings much frost and rain, then January and February will be mild."

"Windy October, dry January."

And February –

"A warm October, a cold February."

Incidentally, the Met Office has declared the period 24th
October to 13th November to be habitually a stormy period,
and October 28th, the feasts of Sts Simon and Jude, would
appear to uphold this: it is claimed that there is never a year
without rain on this day. Hallowe'en, 31st, is the only
exception to the rule, having a reputation for being a quiet
night.

There is a great deal of good, sound matter in the October
forecast signs. They fit in well with the Days of Prediction and
they should all be taken seriously. Together, they form the
best long term forecasts known to us.

* * * * * *

November

Many people call this the Black Month, though John Clare, the
Northamptonshire poet, wrote about it –

"Sybil of months and worshipper of winds,
I love thee, rude and boisterous as thou art."

November's Day of Prediction is 11th, St Martin's Day, sometimes called Martlemas Day. There are a number of other days with sayings attached to them: the 1st (All Saints); the 10th (Martinmas Eve); the 23rd (St Clement) and the 25th (St Catherine). The 6th to 13th will be cold according to Buchan, the 15th to 21st will be quiet according to the Met Office and the same authority states that the 24th to 14th December will be a stormy period. Buchan was one of the few forecasters who has left his mark on the world. Born in 1829, the son of a Scots weaver, he started life as a schoolmaster. In due course, he gave up teaching to study the weather. He discovered, and gave his name to, Buchan's Cold Periods and Buchan's Warm Periods. The Cold Periods, five in number, occur in April, May, June, August and November. The three Warm Periods occur in July, August and December. Buchan very boldly gave specific dates to them; nevertheless, they will be found to be surprisingly accurate in Scotland and the English Border counties, though less so further south.

Here are the references to the dates in November.

All Saints 1st November

"On 1st November if weather is clear
'Tis the end of the sowing you'll do for the year."

– In other words, the weather will deteriorate thereafter with rain or frost.

Martinmas Eve 10th November

> "Where the wind blows on Martinmas Eve, there 't'will
> be for the rest of the winter."

– It is not clear why the saying refers to Martinmas Eve rather
than St Martin's Day – the latter is more likely to be correct.

Martinmas, and *St Martin's little summer* 11th November

> "At any time after Martinmas a short spell of fine,
> warm weather can be expected."

– This contrasts with Buchan, who predicts a cold spell from
9th to 14th.

> "The weather on St Martin's Day foretells the weather
> for three months."

– St Martin is, of course, a Day of Prediction, but it is the only
one which boasts the ability to foretell for three months.

> "Wind North West at Martinmas, a severe winter to
> come."

– If the Martinmas Eve saying is believed then this one will not be surprising. It is reinforced by one from Herefordshire –

"If leaves fall not by Martinmas Day, a cruel winter's on the way."

St Clement's Day 23rd

"St Clement gives the winter."

– Notice the positive tone of this old saw. St Clement is a reliable saint who will usually predict the winter to come with fair accuracy.

"Very inClement weather!"

St Catherine's Day 25th (again, a very reliable saint!)

> "As St Catherine, foul or fair,
> So 't'will be next Febryair."

That completes the minor days of prediction for the month, but there are several other old sayings which have stood the test of time.

> "November cold, Christmas warm."

— This one is sometimes right, but there would appear to be a degree of wishful thinking about it.

> "If ice in November will bear a duck,
> The rest of the winter is slush and muck."

— Very true, one can put one's shirt on it! Put in another way, it is sometimes rendered —

> "Ice in November brings mud in December."

Or, as they express it in Germany —

> "If the water freezes in November, January will be all
> the wetter."

The Forecast is . . .

Now for a very old and truly delightful one –

> "If the November goose wishbone be thick, so will the
> winter weather be; if thin, likewise the winter weather."

– So start feeling the wishbones of your geese about now!

For the more modern predictions we have Buchan's Cold Period, 6th to 13th; the Met Office quiet period, 15th to 21st; and their stormy period, 24th November to 14th December.

November is a miserable month. The weather is deteriorating, the sun's arc gets daily ever lower, and the evenings are closing in. As the poet Thomas Hood put it –

"No warmth, no cheerfulness, no healthful ease,
No comfortable feel in any member,
No shade, no shine, no butterflies, no bees,
No fruit, no flowers, no leaves, November!"

* * * * * *

December

The best piece of advice about this month is given in an old saying dating from the 18th century – "In December, keep yourself warm and sleep" – if only one could! Apart from Buchan's Warm Period of 3rd to 14th and the Met Office stormy period from 25th to 31st, there are only two dates to remember in the month: St Thomas's Day, 21st, which is a Day of Prediction, and New Year's Eve. There are some predictions attached to Christmas Day, but as I said before, the probability is that they ought to refer to St Thomas' Day, summed up in the jingle –

"St Thomas Day is always grey; the longest night, the shortest day."

"If it freeze on St Thomas' Day, the price of corn will fall. If it be mild, the price will rise."

– So hope for a cold day if you want a fine summer!

"A dull Christmas Day with no sun bodes ill for the harvest."

– But they seem to think otherwise in Germany; their favourite Christmas Forecast is – "Stormy weather at Christmas gives plenty of fruit next year."

Here are a few others –

"If Christmas Day on a Thursday be
A windy winter we shall see." (Norfolk)

"A black Christmas brings a full churchyard."

"A green Christmas brings a good harvest next year."

"When the sun shines through the apple trees on Christmas Day,
When autumn comes, they will a load of fruit display."

"If ice bears before Christmas, it won't bear a goose afterwards."

New Year's Eve has a jingle which is always reliable –

"If on New Year's Eve the wind blows South
It betokeneth warmth and growth.
If West, much milk and fish in the sea.

If North, cold and storms there will be.

If East, the trees will bear much fruit.

If North East, then flee it, man and beast (brute?)."

Finally, a gem from Pliny. The period 23rd to 31st was known in his day as the Halcyon Days. According to Pliny, a spell of tranquil weather was ordained by the gods around the time of the Winter Solstice, to enable the halcyon birds (kingfishers) to build floating nests on the sea. They needed calm to rear their young!

Pliny is strongly contested by the Met Office, who have labelled the period 25th to 31st as a stormy one. Perhaps they order things differently in the Mediterranean.

* * * * * *

January

It has been said, and said recently, that any government worth its salt, would abolish January and February by law. Politicians being what they are, this has sadly never been put into effect!

By far the most important date this month is St Paul's Day, 25th, mentioned in the last chapter, but all that has gone before in this chapter may be used to test and reinforce St Paul's predictions.

"The blackest month of all the year.
It is the month of Janivier."

– Those words were written before the days of Income Tax
Final Demands, but they are quoted here to prove how sound
these sayings are, even in a modern context. Final Demands
and Christmas overdrafts certainly make it a very black month,
and weatherwise it is usually no less unpleasant. For instance
– "As the days lengthen, does the cold strengthen" – too true.
One event is certain: about this time there will be at least one
very cold snap, very likely with snow. It has been known to
arrive as early as Boxing Day and as late as 30th January. But
early or late, be sure it will come, and it will probably be the
worst cold snap of the year. The longest that it has been
known to last in living memory was ten weeks. There is some
truth in the saying that the hardest winters are those that start
around Twelfth Night, following a dry December. One point
about snow, generally unknown and worth recording here: if
snow lies for three days it will require another fall of snow to
take it away.

Here is another prediction, and a reliable one at that – "In
January if the sun appear, March and April will pay full dear."
And from Lancashire – "A dry and frosty Janiveer is like to
make a plenteous year" – Since a warm, fine January is almost
always followed by a foul March and April, with a late spring,
you can depend on this saying.

If you have a vineyard, take heed of the following warning

from Germany – "If January is wet the barrels stay empty." And if you are a farmer, take heed of this – it is wise to plan your hay crop now. If the grass is already starting to grow, then do not look for two hay crops in the summer, for the earlier it starts, the worse it will be later on, and vice versa.

> "If grass do grow in Janiveer,
> 'T'will grow the worse for all the year."

Many farmers rely on this saying totally. An old Latin tag, which has been translated into a jingle supports it – "If Janivier Calends be summerly gay, 't'will winter continue to Calends of May." The Calends was, of course, the Latin word for the 1st of the month, in this case, New Year's Day. Nottinghamshire puts it another way – "Janivier Spring, worth nothing" – but it all adds up to the same thing: if there is any good weather in January, we will pay for it later on! No wonder the Romans named it after Janus, the two-faced god – the smiling face is the treacherous one.

I referred in Chapter One to St Paul's Day. Apparently, it is also St Annanias' Day – too many saints, too few days! It is said that clouds on St Annanias' Day portend floods.

> "If St Annanias' Day be fair and clear,
> It betokeneth a happy year.
> But if it chance to snow or rain
> Dear will be all sorts of grain.

If clouds or mist do dark the sky
Great store of birds and beasts will die.
And if the winds do fly aloft
Then wars shall vex the Kingdom oft."

– A nice month, isn't it? However, there is one day when good weather may be foretold, St Vincent's Day, 22nd. There are two old jingles concerning it.

"St Vincent's Day if the sky is clear,
More wine than water will crown the year."

Or, should you be a teetotaller, you may prefer –

"Remember on St Vincent's Day,
If the sun his beams display,
'Tis a token bright and clear
Of prosperous weather throughout the year."

In one version there is another line inserted between the second and third, which runs – "Be sure to mark the transient gleam." It seems to imply that just a glimmer of sunshine is enough to sustain St Vincent's prophecy. The saint has one further word of wisdom to add – "If the birds start singing on St Vincent's Day, 't'will be an early Spring." St Vincent is the only prophet with anything cheerful to tell us!

The following are some quaint prognostications which I

first learnt in Co Durham, but I confess that I have never put them to the test –

"January 8th weather before noon foretells June weather, afternoon that of May.

January 9th weather before noon foretells August weather, afternoon that of July.

January 10th, weather before noon foretells October, afternoon that of September.

January 11th weather before noon foretells December, afternoon that of November.

January 13th foretells the weather for the whole year."

(Lloyd, 1590)

There is also an East Anglian saying which states that the first three days in January rule the coming months.

To conclude, I have one more gloomy prognostication – "A wet January, a wet Spring." You may also like to note the forecasting of the latter day prophets, the Met Office: 5th to 17th will be stormy; 18th to 24th will be quiet; 25th to 31st will be stormy again – which appears to wrap the month up nicely.

So, the dates to note in January are the 1st (Calends), the 22nd and 25th; also, if you will, the 8th to 13th. It is better to

leave the month with its horrid reputation, well summed up in
the phrase –

"Janivier, freeze the pot upon the fire."

Chapter Four

THE MONTHLY SIGNS – 2
The Summer Forecast Months

The next four months of the year, February to May, have their sights set for shorter ranges and embrace the run-up to the harvest, extending from June to September. The harvest includes hay-making, the corn harvest and the fruit crop, the staple products of the agriculturist. The farmer lives by what he produces and, broadly speaking, these are the only months of the year when he produces anything from the soil.

Let us start with an old Kentish saying – "February always brings the rain, and thaws the frozen lakes again." So, if you are to have a good summer, alas, February will need to be a cold, wet, miserable month. As the saying ordains – "All the months of the year curse a fair Februair."

Turning to the subject of crops we have – "If February brings no rain, 'tis neither good for grass nor grain." In the same vein comes the following from Gloucestershire –

> "Warm February – light hay crop
> Cold February – heavy hay crop."

Thankfully there are some cheerful sayings as well –"Much February snow April summer doth show." Put another way, this runs – "In February if thou hearest thunder, thou shalt see a summer wonder." Conflictingly, it is also said – "Dry February, dry Summer." And there is another rather ambiguous one, which goes – "A warm day in February is a dream of Summer." Is this a forecast or just a pious hope? Interpret it as you will. Contrariwise, another popular saying is – "February Spring ain't worth a pin."

Back in October it was predicted that a warm October meant a cold February. But in November St Catherine dictated the February weather with the words – "As St Catherine, foul or fair, so 't'will be next Februair."

There are two more predictions for Candlemas Day (2nd February), in addition to those given in Chapter One. First –

"On Candlemas Day if thorns be a-drop
You can be sure of a good pea crop."

– Peas mature ready for picking about June, which implies good weather about then.

The second is a typical one from the West Country –

"If Candlemas Day do bluster and blow
Winter be over, as all do well know."

A recent discovery from Nottinghamshire runs as follows –

"If Candlemas be wet with rain,
Winter's gone and won't come again.
If Candlemas be bright and fair,
You've half the winter to come and mair."

Northamptonshire provides a variation on this –

"If Candlemas Day be dull and grey, unsaddle your
horse and give him some hay.
If Candlemas Day be fair and gay, unsaddle your horse
and turn him away."

There is another general saying, concerning St Valentine's Day, 14th February. I confess I have never put this one to the test, but for what it is worth, I pass it on here –

"If she be a good goose, her dame well to pay,
She'll lay two good eggs afore Valentine's Day."

– So when you have finished feeling your goose's wishbone, remind her of this saying. There would be no harm in hinting at the alternative!

Finally, St Mattias' Day, 24th – "St Mattee sends the sap up the tree" – This is not the meaningless saying that it might seem: the date is the usual time for the sap to start rising and helps to determine whether or not there will be an early spring. The prophets again come to our assistance: Buchan declares that the period 7th to 14th will be cold, and the Met Office says that 24th to 28th will be stormy.

To conclude this cheerless month, here is one last ancient saw –

> "February Filldyke, be it black or be it white;
> But if it be white, 'tis better to like."

* * * * * *

March

March is known as the month of winds and new life, bringing a pleasant change for the forecaster, as some of the signs actually speak of good weather in the future. So let's start with these – "A dry, cold March never begs its bread."– In other words, a good grain harvest implies a dry July and August. In the same vein – "A peck of March dust is worth a king's ransom." Others include –

> "A peck of March dust and a shower in May
> Makes the corn green and the meadows all gay."

> "March dust to be sold, worth a ransom in gold."

"A dry March and a rainy April makes a beautiful May."

"A showery March and a showery May portend a wholesome summer, if there be a showery April in between."

"March, month of many weathers, wildly comes
In hail and snow and threatening floods and hums."
(John Clare)

"A windy March foretells a fine May."

"He always sings in the rain!"

Now for the bad news, here are two reliable sayings about late frosts – "A mist in March is a frost in May", and "So many fogs in March, so many frosts in May"– So count the March fogs with care, especially if you are a fruit grower.

Watch out for wet weather, too – "A wet March makes a sad harvest." And, in more detail – "March damp and warm will do farmers much harm." Continuing the theme – "March flowers make no Summer bowers." For the last of the bad news we have – "March snow hurts the seed."

March 21st is St Benedict's Day, the vernal equinox and a Day of Prediction. It is said that as the wind is on that day, so it will remain for three months. St Benedict's also foretells the weather, though for a variable period, up to Good Friday, the next Day of Prediction.

A forecast which I have found to have a high degree of accuracy runs as follows – "As the weather is on Shrove Tuesday, so 't'will be till the end of Lent."– They also say that a dry Lent spells a fertile year.

Turning again to farming we have – "March dry, good rye." 1st March, St David's Day, carries this note – "Ever upon St David's Day put oats and barley in the clay." St Benedict has some further advice for us – "On St Benedict's Day sow thy peas or keep them in the nick."

2nd March is St Chad's Day, and it reveals this gem – "Every goose lays before St Chad, whether a good goose or a bad." – So, if your goose has not laid by St Chad's Day start fattening her up for the pot, for she is no good as a layer! Last month I spoke of geese laying before St Valentine's Day, but the reference was to "good geese". St Chad speaks of all geese, whether good or bad. These last few tags are very significant. They offer signs by which one can gauge whether the season will be early or late, and they should not be ignored.

Moles are a good guide to the future weather, but only for the short term of a fortnight or so. When they start to be active, particularly in spring, it is a sure sign that warmer weather is on its way. But be warned: when it comes it may only last a short time. Field mice scurrying about, on the other hand, are a prelude to bad weather: they are laying in stocks of food.

Turning now to the more general signs, we have – "If you've March in Janivier, Janivier in March I fear" and "After a frosty Winter there will be a good fruit harvest" – which is particularly worth noting. A frosty Winter delays the setting of the blossom till after the last frost, and also tends to kill off some of the insects which attack the fruit trees. It is also said that March borrows its last week from April, which is true insofar that the tail end of the month is often more spring-like than the rest of it.

Finally, a saying that is known to all and sundry – "If March comes in like a lion it will go out like a lamb" (and vice versa) – which is quite dependable as long as you bear in mind that it usually only applies to the first and last two or three days of the month.

March tends to be the driest month of the year, though it is subject to cold snaps and frosts. The third week of the month is often the driest in the whole year. It is interesting to note that our forebears used to say that March was the first month of the year, as it was the first month when winter really showed signs of retreat. Sound thinkers, our forebears! The 21st, St Benedict's Day, used to be the legal start of the year.

Just a few more thoughts before we leave the month –

"The March sun raiseth but it disolveth not."

"Better bitten by a snake than feel the sun in March."

And if you are elderly –

"February search, March try.
April says whether you live or die."

But let us finish on a cheerful note. They say in Northamptonshire that –

"If March comes in all stormy and black,
She carries the winter away on her back."

Goodbye March.

* * * * * *

"April and May are the keys to the whole year."

April is the first really cheerful month of the year. The flowers begin to appear and we all start to experience that wonderful uplift of spirit that Nature brings us with the spring. A young man's fancy, the poet tells us, lightly turns to thoughts of love. The young woman's, we must presume, has been turned that way all through the winter! But nevertheless it is a fine, optimistic month. As the old song put it – "Spring is busting out all over."

Starting at the beginning of the month we learn that –

"Should it rain on All Fools' Day
It brings good crops of corn and hay."

Few people are actually aware of the origin of All Fools Day, with its cry of "April Fool". New Year's Day originally fell on April 1st, but was later altered to St Benedict's Day, 21st March. Those who forgot and who still wished their friends a Happy New Year on April 1st were greeted with the words "April Fool".

Most of the old saws have it that it is best to have a wet April, so here is a fair selection –

"When April blows his horn,
'Tis good for hay and corn."

"April cold and wet,
Fills the barns best yet."

"A cold April brings both bread and wine."

"After a cold April the barns fill well."

"April wet, good wheat." (Yorkshire)

"April rain makes large sheaves." (Worcestershire)

"April showers bring May flowers."

"East wind in Spring a brilliant summer will bring."

"If April brings a lot of rain it augurs well." (Germany)

As a general rule, however, the April weather is a mixture of all sorts, as in the words of the old Norfolk saying – "April weather, rain and sunshine together." For the last of the general predictions for the month remember – "Thunder in Spring the cold will bring." To sum up: we must suffer a cold, wet April if we want a good summer.

Now to consider Easter, which as we all know, is a moveable feast, falling sometimes in March but usually in April; for this reason I give the sayings here. There are many forecasts which concern this period, and they are singularly dependable. As I said before, New Year's Day was originally celebrated on 1st March, and later altered to 1st April. Since neither of these dates had any real significance, a final shift was made to 21st March, the Vernal Equinox. Now primitive man worshipped the Sun, the giver of life and heat; but being one to hedge his bets, he also worshipped the Sun's wife, the Moon. Eastre, as she was known to the Saxons, soon needed her own special day on which to be glorified and what better day than the first full moon after the start of the new year? And so it was. Christian priests, knowing that old customs die hard and also recognizing the great importance of the day, were quick to adopt the festival as theirs, changing only the day to the first Sunday after the first full moon after St Benedict's Day. The original Day of Prediction was probably that full moon, which is likely to occur a few days before Good Friday. So, as the change in the weather will most likely come a few days after the change in the moon, the Day of Prediction is as near to Good Friday as we can tell.

Hedging one's bets

The following are the most reliable sayings –

"If on Palm Sunday there be rain, that betokeneth to goodness. If it thunder on that day, then it signifieth a merrie year." – The source of this old saying is not known for sure, but it is generally believed to have come from *The New Book of Knowledge*,.

"Rain on Good Friday and Easter Day
 A good year for grass a bad year for hay." – Note well the word "and". It must rain on BOTH Easter and Good Friday for the prophecy to hold good, and you will find that it very seldom does so."
"If the sun shine on Easter Day, so it will shine on Whitsunday."

"The weather on Easter Days foretells the harvest."

Moving further along the year we come to Whitsuntide.

"If it happened to rain on Whitsunday much thunder and lightning would follow." – I query the word "much", some thunder, yes, but much is doubtful.

"Spring has come when you can put your foot on seven daisies in your lawn."

– This once brought forth an irresistible crack from an old Devon gardener I knew: "If yeu gotten one o'thik yur modern larns wi' no daisies, looks like spring won't niver come to 'ee."

Sometimes a prolonged winter seems to turn into summer overnight, a phenomenon which is covered by the saying – "When winter meets summer it foretells a hot, dry summer." I should also include here a quote from that brilliant sage, Sir Thomas More, whose head Queen Elizabeth I removed. They are wise words, pay them due heed – "The weather in the second half of April foretells the summer."

An old saw about the Blackthorn Winter, 11th to 14th April, which coincides exactly with Buchan's Cold Period runs – "Just as the blackthorn is coming into blossom, expect a cold snap."– This is reliable as far as the blossom is concerned, be it early or be it late. But the dates may vary with early or late springs. The blackthorn gives another signal, too. If it blooms before the leaves appear, be sure that there will be a bitter spell – perhaps even snow.

And to conclude on a more cheerful note –

"Greenfly at Easter, June will blister."

* * * * * *

May

The ancient sages were nothing if not pessimistic, and who can blame them, seeing that they were dealing with the English climate? Just in case it might be thought that summer has come in with the month of May, remember this one –

> "Ne'er cast a clout till May be out,
> Button to chin till June be in,
> If you change in June you change too soon,
> Change in July? You'll catch cold bye and bye.
> Change in August if you must.
> But be sure to remember, change back in September."

"N'er cast a clout ..."

84

– Our forebears were adamant about this. In Lincolnshire they used to say that you should not change your clothes "until the cuckoo picks up dirt". The lines are attributed to Andrew Bell. But there is another similarly cautionary tag – "Who doffs his coat on a winter's day, will gladly put it on in May."

A saying of doubtful veracity runs – "He who would live for ever must eat sage in May" – which has nothing to do with the weather but it provokes thought.

If you are looking for a good summer, the best May weather for you will be cold and rainy –

"A cold May and windy a full barn will find ye."
(Thomas Turner, 1530)

"Rain in May makes bread and corn."

"Cold, wet May, good for corn and hay."

"A wet May means a dry September." (Suffolk)

"A cold May brings bread for the whole year." (Poland)

"Rain in May for long hay."

Not all the prophets concur however. For example – "A dry May foretells a wholesome summer." – This one seems to contradict all the others, and it is supported by – "Flowers in May, good cocks of hay."

The next one seems to compromise between the two points of view: it takes two forms in different parts of the country.

"Mist in May, heat in June
Puts the harvest right in tune."

"A leaky May and a dry June
Makes the harvest come right soon."

Other harvest forecasts include – "Rain in May makes plenty of hay," – but watch that it is not too leaky, for – "A May flood never did anyone any good."

A May flood never did anyone any good

"Come on, Mabel, let's get out of here"

Also – "Who sows oats in May has little to repay." And – "A swarm of bees in May is worth a load of hay."

May is usually the month when the bees become active. They give clear weather signals, if you are near enough to observe them, as the following verse explains –

> "When the bees all leave their hive
> Then it's good to be alive.
> When they all go home again
> Then it's surely going to rain."

Here is one sign which has never let me down –

> "When the mulberry tree begins to shoot, the last frost
> has gone."

A final pointer for this month is a saying that I have heard in the South of England but nowhere further north. I am a little doubtful as to its accuracy, so please treat it with caution –

> "Spring will not settle in properly until the cowslips
> have died down."

May has always been a difficult month for the soothsayer, one gains the impression that whoever said the sooths was determined to foretell a good summer, whatever the May weather! It should nevertheless be classed as an uncertain month, which is regrettable, as all the previous ones have been so positive. It is also the last of the months with a claim to forecast the long term weather; the thoughts of the farmer must now turn to the more immediate future.

Chapter Five

THE MONTHLY SIGNS - 3
The Harvest Months

The months of June to September are the all-important ones for the agriculturalist. His income for the year depends on the harvest, starting with the hay crop in May or June, followed by the corn crop in high summer, and finishing with the fruit crop towards Autumn. Bad weather, even a short spell, can have disastrous effects on the crops, and ruin a whole year's work. So the farmer's anxieties – and the signs he must look out for – concern the short term of days or weeks rather than months.

June

Where would our popular song writers be without June to rhyme with soon, spoon and tune? It has ever been so. For instance –

"A dripping June keeps all in tune."

"Calm weather in June, sets all in tune."

"A leaky June brings harvest soon."

"A swarm of bees in June is worth a silver spoon."

There are a number of important dates in June, the first being –

"If on 8th of June it rain,
It tells of a wet harvest, men sayin'."

The next, and far more important, is the Day of Prediction, the 15th, St Vitus Day of which there is the aforementioned –

"If St Vitus Day be rainy weather
'Twill rain for forty days together."

– Note carefully that it refers to "rainy weather", not just a shower. Knowing our English weather, you need to interpret the phrase somewhat liberally.

The next significant day is St John's Day, 24th June, Midsummer Day, for which the sayings are numerous. As well as those included in Chapter One, there is –

"Before St John's Day we pray for rain, afterwards we get it anyway."

"If the cuckoo sings after St John's Day, the harvest will be late." (Always dependable.)

"If Midsummer Day be ever so little rainy, the hazel and walnut will be scarce, and corn smitten in many places; but apples, pears and plums will not be hurt." (Wiltshire, *Shepherd's Almanac*, written in the 17th Century)

"If it rains on Midsummer Day the filberts will be spoilt." (Filbert farmers, note carefully!)

"Cut your thistles before St John,
Or you'll have two instead of one."

The remaining noteworthy date is 11th, St Barnabas Day, for which there are a number of sayings.

"Barnaby bright, all day and no night." – This is quite a good one to rely on: I have found St Barnabas' Day is nearly always a a fine clear day.
"St Barnabas, mow your first grass." – The saying comes from the Midlands, so areas North and South should adjust appropriately. This, of course, refers to hay field grass. Lawns may be mown earlier, sometimes even in March.

"When Barnabas smiles both night and day
Poor ragged robin blooms in the hay." – In other
words, it is a great time for weed growth. Ask any
gardener!

This is the last of the sayings associated with dates in the
month. Here are a few less specific –

"If there are thunderstorms in June, there will be a
plump harvest." (Germany)

"June damp and warm does the farmer no harm."

"Good summer brings hard winter."

"If a hard winter is followed by a poor summer, the
following winter will be harder still."

– These latter two are almost infallible. Here is another
dependable one –

"If the cuckoo delays changing his tune until mid-June,
St Swithin's Day will be wet."

You will recall the old jingle about the cuckoo (see Chapter on
Birds) that "in June he changes his tune"; he changes his call
from a straight "cuckoo" to a stuttering "Cuck-cuckoo". Very
occasionally you will hear him give two preliminary "cucks".

When he does so you are in for a particularly fine spell.

A modern one now: Wimbledon fortnight, which embraces the last week in June and the first in July, is nearly always fine. It coincides with Buchan's Cold Period, June 29th to July 14th.

But just before we leave "Flaming" June, a word of warning: don't be deceived by that adjective. June usually has more wet days than any other month. How often does one hear of a wet Ascot and cricket matches rained off? It could properly be called the Wet Month.

* * * * * *

July

There are very few predictions arising from the month of July as hay-making and harvest are by now in full swing. Buchan foretells that 12th to 15th will be warm, and there is of course that most well-known of Prediction Days – St Swithin's Day, 15th July. As well as the rather depressing saying concerning the amount of rain to follow, there is the more cheerful –

> "If it rains on St Swithin's Day, the saint is christening the apples, and they will be sweet and plentiful."

An old Devon saying which may apply more to the West Country than to the country as a whole runs –

"If the first of July be rainy weather
'T'will rain for full four weeks together."

But here is a more optimistic one from Monmouthshire, which is certainly true in its county of origin –

"Watch the weather from 4th to 16th July. If it is fine and summery, the rest of the summer is likely to be fine."

Gardeners always watch the behaviour of wild flowers, or at least the wise ones do –

"When the goat's beard" – otherwise known as Johnny-go-to-bed-at-noon – "closes its flowers before midday, there is rain in the air.
If it stays late with its petals open, the atmosphere is dry and the weather set fair."

The humble clover is even better. No matter if the sky is clear and the glass rising, when the clover leaves are shut and are pointing to the sky, reach for your brolly. Pay attention also to the Welsh poppy and the rock rose: both will anticipate rain by hanging their heads.

Three last words for the farmer –

"A shower in July when the corn begins to fill
Is worth a plough of oxen and all that
Belongs theretill."

"In July cut your rye."

"A swarm of bees in July is not even worth a fly."

Finally, from Germany a saying which is so very true of this country –

"What is to thrive in September must be baked in July."

– I wonder why we have never evolved an English equivalent. So much for July.

* * * * * *

August

As well as being the Day of Prediction, St Bartholomew's Day is the most important day, and, appropriately, it has a number of sayings (see Chapter One).

95

"St Bartholomew's brings the cold dew." – A point to be borne in mind by campers!

Gardeners should also note that this is the day when delicate plants should be brought indoors, and that –

"St Bartholomew's is the day to start collecting honey."

The 1st August is Lammas' Day (Loafmas). The name derives from the Anglo-Saxon custom of offering the first fruits of harvest on that day.

"After Lammas the corn ripens as much by night as by day."

Remember also the 6th, the Feast of the Transfiguration, explained in Chapter One.

For general predictions we have –

"August fills the barn and September the loft."

"Dry August and warm does the farmer no harm."

"A wet, rainy August makes a hard bread crust."

But, on the other hand – "Too much August sun disappoints the maid, the priest and the host, for it scorches up all vegetables."

As usual, the Germans have an apt saying for the month, but in this case it appears more monitory than prophetic – "What is not cooked in August will be spoiled in September."

The moist sultry days of the year are reckoned to be the Dog Days, a period of twenty days before and twenty days after the rising of the Dog Star Sirius. If we are to have a summer at all, this is the most likely time: roughly from mid-July to the end of August, or corn harvest time. Sirius is the brightest star in the heavens, and is one of those in the southern constellation, Canis Major.

A certain amount of damp is essential this month – "August needs the dew as much as men need bread." Of the dog days, it is said – "If the dog days be clear 't'will be fine all the year."

There is little in the way of predictions for the month, apart from Buchan's prediction of a warm period from the 12th to 15th. The reason is not far to seek. We are nearing the end of the farmer's year and he is not too bothered about what is going to happen after September. As I said before, all "natural" weather forecasting is geared to the anxieties of the husbandman, and is little concerned with the interests of the ordinary citizen.

And to finish with another wise saying from Germany – "A warm Autumn is usually followed by a long Winter."

September

Like August, September has very little in the way of sage predictions. Its one Day of Prediction, 29th, St Michael's Day, is also a Quarter Day. Note, incidentally, that each Quarter Day is a Day of Wind Prediction.

There are, however, two long term predictions, both of rather uncertain veracity –

> "If acorns abound in September, snow will be deep in December."

> "As the weather is in September, so 't'will be in March."

St Michael has two more sayings associated with his Day – "A fine Michaelmas sets all in tune" – In other words, it foretells fine weather until Martinmas. And – "On Michaelmas Day the devil puts his foot on blackberries."

Of September 1st, St Giles' Day, there is a very optimistic saying – "Fair on September 1st, fair for the month." – In actual fact, this is a most unpredictable month and one should not be quick to jump to conclusions. On the other hand, the Meteorological Office might agree: its warm period runs from 1st to 17th.

St Matthew's Day, 21st, follows shortly, of which it is said – "St Matthew brings the cold, rain and dew." It is also said that St Matthew "shuts up" the bees, which I can believe as they certainly don't like cold weather. For those of you more observant of plants than insects, the end of summer may be heralded by the foxgloves and hollyhocks shedding their leaves.

The strong winds start during this month, and will reach their peak about the time of the equinox on 21st. The actual date on which they start varies greatly, sometimes as early as 2nd and sometimes as late as 24th. This has given rise to the ancient prayer – "September blow soft till the fruit's in the loft."

To conclude this rather cruel month, and indeed our year, here are some more general sayings –

"The summer goes with the swallows." – which is true, whether they fly away early or late.

"When summer meets winter it is a good augury for the coming Spring."

"September dries up the wells and breaks down the bridges."

"If bunches of nuts do hang on the branches after leaf fall, it betokens a frosty winter with much snow."

Chapter Six

Signs of Rain

"Is it going to rain today?" This question is quite the commonest in the English language. The tone may be light-hearted, but the possibility of rain is no laughing matter. It is of solemn and serious concern to everyone. So how can one tell for sure whether or not it is going to rain?

There must be hundreds of signs all around us which can answer the question. No attempt has been made to record them all here, for one thing space would not allow it, but an effort has been made to give examples from as wide a range as possible. Always remember that your own knowledge and observation is a valuable supplement to the signs given here.

The first and most obvious signs are to be found in the sky, and nearly everyone will have some knowledge of what to look for here. When the sun blazes from a cloudless sky on a still day, we don't expect rain. When low, black clouds drive in from the south-west, we do. Other signs vary from one part of the country to another, and only the vaguest generalisations can apply to the country as a whole. The solution is to learn the cloud signs in your part of the world and rely on your own judgement.

"It ain't gonna rain no more."

Let us start with what is probably the best-known old saw –

"Red sky at night, shepherd's delight;
Red sky at morning, shepherd's warning."

– The origin on the other hand, of this most reliable of sayings is unknown, though it may have been an ancient book entitled *The Country Calendar,* or *The Shepherd of Bunbury's Rules,* of which copies are now, sadly, rare. It is interesting to note that it is not the oldest reference to a red sky at night. Turning to the Bible we find in St Matthew's Gospel, Chapter 16, Verses 2 and 3 –

> "When it is evening ye say, it will be fair weather for the sky is red. And in the morning, it will be rough weather today, for the sky is red and louring."

There are more sayings peculiar to the summer months. Here are three which I have found most reliable –

> "Dew falling by night, the next day will be bright."

> "Summer mist at dawn, the next day will be warm."

> "Sun shining through shower, won't last half an hour."

It is nice to find sayings which forecast fine weather, so if you are now feeling happier, here is one to bring you back to earth again – "Rain from the East, lasts three days at least." And one which has some good news and bad, depending on your circumstances – "Rain before seven, stop before eleven." The source of this latter is unknown, though I can vouch for its reliability. The meteorological explanation lies in the fact that a typical rain-bearing warm front tends to be about two hundred miles wide – travelling across country at between twenty-five and fifty miles per hour it takes about four to six hours to cross a given point; so, if well established by seven it has a good chance of clearing up before eleven.

Here is one from Suffolk which is often correct – "If it rains when the sun is shining, it will rain at the same time next day." And some from various locations, of varying reliability –

"The farther the view the nearer the rain." – usually correct.

"A ring around the sun spells rain." – very true.

"When the wind goes round to the north-west the rain ceases." – what a comforting piece of news! It is also often true.

Turning now to some longer extracts, here is an old piece of doggerel which has a number of local variations, but runs much as follows –

"When the dew is on the grass
Rain will never come to pass.
If grass be dry at morning light
Expect the rain before the night.
If red the sun before his race

Be sure the rain will fall apace.
When the wind is from the hill
Then good weather it will spoil.
When the mist is from the sea
Then good weather it will be.
When the wind is in the East
Rain for several days at least.
When clouds appear like rocks and towers
The earth's refreshed with frequent showers.
If the sun in red should set
The next day surely won't be wet.
If the sun should set in grey
The next will be a rainy day."

There is another delightful one, which applies specially to fishermen –

"When the wind is in the North
The skilful fisher goes not forth.
When the wind is in the South
It blows the bait in the fish's mouth.
When the wind is in the West
Fishing is at its very best.
When the wind is in the East
'Tis good for neither fish nor beast." (Wiltshire.)

John Clare gives us a delightful poem in his *Shepherd's Calendar* –

"And scarlet, starry points of flowers,
Pimpernel, dreading nights and showers,
Oft called the shepherd's weather glass,
That sleeps till suns have died the grass,
Then wakes and spreads its creeping bloom
Till clouds with threatening shadows come,
Then close it shuts to sleep again;
Which weeders see and talk of rain,
And boys, that see them shut so soon
Call: 'Johnny, go to bed at noon'."

Thomas Tussler the famous poet (1520-1580), said in his *Description of the Properties of Winds at All times of the Year—*

"North Winds send hail, South Winds bring rain
East Winds bewail, West Winds blow amain;
North-East is too cold, South-East not too warm,
North-West is too bold, South-West doth no harm.

The North is a noyer to grass of all suites,
The East a destroyer to herd and all fruits;
The South, with his showers, refresheth all corn,
The West, to all flowers, may not be foreborne.

The West, as a father, all goodness doth bring,
The East, a forebearer no manner of thing;
The South, as unkind, draweth sickness too near,
The North, as a friend, maketh all again clear.

With temperate wind, we be blessed of God,
With tempest we find we are beat with his rod:
All power, we know, to remain in his hand,
However wind blow, by sea or by land.

Though winds do rage, as winds were wood,
And cause spring tides to raise great flood,
And lofty ships leave anchor in mud,
Bereaving many of life, and of blood;
Yet true it is, as cow chews cud,
And trees, at Spring, do yield forth bud,
Except wind stands, as never it stood,
It is an ill wind turns none to good."

Turning now to insects, much can be learned. Here are a few examples –

"If beetles fly about in the evening, it will be fine next day."

"When midges bite between June and October, wet weather is on the way."

Mouffet's *Theatre of Insects* puts it another way –

"If gnats at sunset do play up and down in open air, they presage heat; but if they altogether sting those that pass by, then cold weather and much rain."

"Spiders' webs on long lines foretell a fine day, but if they shorten the threads it will rain." – This one is totally reliable if only applied to cobwebs out-of-doors in the open air.

"When eager bites the thirsty flea
Clouds and rain you'll surely see." – If you don't believe this one, try it out!

"Bees won't swarm before a near storm."

"Bees won't leave the hive if it is going to rain."

"No flying today!"

Ants tell a similar story: you will never see an ant out of its nest when it is raining. Bees will also predict fine weather – when they fly far from their hives and come home late then the weather is set fair.

There are many more signs to be found amongst the activities of insects, but since they are sometimes difficult to spot, we will turn now to farm and domestic animals. Here is a delightful jingle from Monmouthshire –

> "When the goose and the gander
> Begin to meander,
> Its perfectly plain,
> They're dancing for rain."

– but I must confess that I have not checked it up, so you will need to watch them carefully yourself.

> "When *all* the cattle in a field lie down, heavy rain is
> imminent."

– Be wary of this statement. Though there is some truth in it, herds of cattle tend to graze and to cud together; when cudding, they lie down, so you may see a whole herd lying down, chewing the cud contentedly, on a fine day. If on the other hand the act of lying down coincides with other signs of rain, reach for your brolly!

"When the domestic pussy cat washes industriously NINE times right over the ears, expect rain." (Herefordshire – Cum grano salis?)

"Cats at play, rain today." (Northamptonshire)

"When young colts lie on their backs, it will rain." – Very true.

"When sheep bleat a lot, or skip about, or when they collect in one corner of a field, turning their backs to the wind, rain is coming."

"If geese cackle for no apparent reason, it will rain."

"When pigs run around with straw in their mouths, rain is imminent."

"Strawdinary!"

Here are two old jingles —

"Hark I hear the asses bray
We shall have some rain today."

"If the cock goes a-crowing to bed
He will rise with a watery head."

One other sign to look out for in farm animals: herbivorous animals generally like their grass dry, so when they are seen feeding at an unusual hour, it is probably because they know that rain is on the way.

Turning to birds, the signs are legion. There is scarcely one breed that does not give some sign or other, so they have been given a chapter of this book all to themselves. Just one I will include here: the mistle thrush who sings high in the branches. His words are prophetic — "More rain, more rain."

Trees, too, are indicative of the forthcoming weather. For instance, when rain is imminent, some, noticeably the sycamore and the poplar, will reveal the lighter-coloured underside of their leaves.

Finally, I have included three slightly longer words of warning. The first is a fairly comprehensive piece from *The New Book of Knowledge*.

"If ducks and drakes their wings do flutter high,
Or tender colts upon their backs do lie;
If sheep do bleat or play and skip about
Or swine hie by straw bearing on their snout;
If oxen lick themselves against the hair,
Or grazing kine to feed apace appear;
If cattle bellow, gazing from below,
Or if dogs entrails rumble to and fro;
If doves and pigeons in the evening come,
Later than usual to their dove house home;
If crows and daws do oft themselves be wet,
Or ants or pissmires home apace do get;
If in the dust hens do their pinions shake,
Or by their flocking a great number make;
If swallows fly upon the water low,
Or woodlice seem in armies for to go;
If flies or gnats or fleas infest or bite
Or sting more than their wont by day or night;
If toads hie home or frogs do croak amain,
Or peacocks cry – soon after, LOOK FOR RAIN."

"Be it dry or be it wet,
Nature always pays its debt."

"The rain it raineth every day
Upon the just and unjust fella.
But more upon the just because
The unjust has the just's umbrella."

"You and your computer navigation"

Chapter Seven

The Birds

It is probably true to say that the behaviour of every species of bird has something to teach us about the weather. For the long term prophecies we have the arrival of the swallows, those trusty birds who instinctively and unfailingly know when summer is going to arrive; if it is going to be early they arrive early; if late late. In the short term we have only to watch the pigeons who, refusing to get caught on the ground in wet weather, take refuge in the trees. Occasionally they cut it fine, but they are never caught out. So, if you see a flock of pigeons suddenly fly off into the trees, failing any other apparent cause, the reason is an imminent rain storm. The examples in this chapter are taken from the whole range of British birds, both migratory and resident.

Let's look first at the migratory birds. Of the many migrant species who fly into the country (or out of it), each can be relied upon to undertake its journey at about the same time every year, thus giving a clear indication of the change in season.

. . .We should have gone with the others!

As an instance, the cuckoo is perhaps the best-known migrant, and the date and place of his first arrival is always reported in *The Times*. Sometimes as early as 24th March, sometimes as late as May, the cuckoo will not arrive until spring is here. The old jingle runs –

> "In April come he will,
> In May he sings all day,
> In June he changes his tune,
> In July he prepares to fly,
> In August go he must."

Another old saying runs – "Early cuckoo, dry summer" – so, the earlier he arrives in or before April, the better the summer; the later he arrives, the worse. And with his arrival, rain is sure to follow – in North-East Scotland, a "gowk storm" (very rough weather) coincides with the event. The cuckoo is also credited with powers to foretell rain: it is popularly asserted that if he calls persistently rain is on its way. I should mention, however, that this is at variance with my own experience: I find that when he calls continuously, as he often does in June, it is a sure sign of good weather.

Here is another one, this time from Norfolk –

> "If the cuckoo lights on a bare bough
> Keep your hay and sell your cow.
> But if he lights on the blooming May,
> Keep your cow and sell your hay."

Chaucer is credited with the lines – "On the third of April come the cuckoo and the nightingale." This is a very precise date, with which some may disagree, and it is bound to vary in different parts of the country. What is more important, is that it provides a date by which to judge whether the season is early or late.

The respective dates of arrival of the swallow, swift and marten vary just as much. Their non-arrival foretells a cold snap: their early arrival predicts a warm spring. An ancient pottery jar was discovered some time ago in Greece, delineating a swallow and three people. Each person had a "speech balloon" attached to the mouth, loosely translated as follows: the father's – "Look, a swallow" the mother's – "Ah, fine weather" and the child's – "Now we shall have summer." Evidently they did not know our saying that one swallow does not make a summer!

The departure of the swallows in the autumn does not foretell the early onset of winter with the same certainty. All too often they depart early simply because we are having a miserable summer. Contrarily, the arrival of the geese is a definite sign of the onset of winter, as is the arrival of the fieldfares and redwings. The starlings, on the other hand, usually arrive a few weeks before the cold weather.

The following old saw forms a useful yardstick by which to judge the punctuality or otherwise of other birds –

> "Come it early or come it late
> In May comes surely the rusty corn crake."

The woodcock is also watched carefully in certain parts of the West Country. They say that if he arrives early it is a sign of good weather and a liberal harvest, but if the hay is not gathered before his arrival, his appearance spells rain.

The dates on which some birds moult and change their plumage is another guide to the forthcoming weather. The clearest example of this is the ptarmigan who changes from brown to white plumage at the approach of winter. The earlier the change, the harder the winter. Stoats, weasels and blue hares do the same. The exception to this rule is man (homo sapiens), who wears white flannels in summer and brown tweeds in winter!

British song birds sing to establish their territories when they are about to mate: the date when they start is an indication of the change to warmer weather. There are other long term signs as well. Perhaps one of the best-known concerns the rooks: when they build their nests at the tops of the trees it presages a dry summer; when they build them down below the tops, it presages a wet summer. This prediction holds good until the end of the nesting season, around the end of June.

"Well? ... Up or down?"

More sayings regarding rooks: when they perch high and crowd together, bad weather is on the way; when they hurtle wildly downwards, gales and storms will follow.

Bird calls and song can be very revealing. When the raven is heard at dawn it foretells a fine day, but if the crow calls first, it will be wet. If the heron – hardly a song bird – calls on the wing during the night, expect strong winds. If it stands on the banks of the water for a long time, expect rain.

. . . "All together now. . ."

Another old saying, invariably reliable, runs – "When owls hunt in daylight in Autumn, there will be a hard winter."

Robins, those most common of garden birds, give an infallible sign as to the quality of the coming winter. During the summer months they live and nest in trees, but in winter they like to establish territories close to dwelling houses, with a view to feeding on scraps and crumbs. This move usually occurs about the second half of September, but before a hard winter it will happen up to a month earlier. The signal to watch for is robins fighting close to the house, and especially near the bird table. An old jingle runs –

"When the robin sings in the bush
Expect the weather to be coarse.
But when the robin sings in the barn
Then the weather will be warm."

Recently I heard of another sign said to foretell the quality of the winter. My informant told me that if the birds strip the trees of their berries in November or December, the winter will be a mild one. But if they leave them on the trees until after Christmas, hard weather should be expected. The theory is that, knowing the ground will be frozen or covered with snow, they leave their stock of food where they can get at it. It is an interesting theory, but one that I have not had time to confirm or prove. I pass it on here as it was given to me, and I would be very interested indeed to learn readers' opinions about it. It may be an explanation of the widely held belief, mentioned in a later chapter, that the size of the crop of holly berries at Christmas is an indication of the coming winter.

The ancients firmly believed in these old sayings about birds, for it was thought then that a bird's ability to fly enabled it to communicate with the powers of the sky. The peacock's cry, for instance, was said to be the sound of approaching rain, and for this gift, the species was greatly revered in South-East Asia. Similarly, in the Shetland Islands the voice of the Black and Red-Throated Diver, known as the Rain Goose, is said to be heard only before bad weather. The mistle thrush, sometimes called the Storm Cock, seems to be stimulated by approaching storms and calls lustily before and during bad weather. The green woodpecker, sometimes called the rainbird, "only calls, or laughs, before rain." (Hampshire.) And when seabirds come far inland it is a sure sign of stormy weather on the coast; the old jingle tells us –

"Seagull, seagull stay on the strand,
It's never good weather when you're inland."

Other signs of rain include: if ducks and geese and other water fowl utter loud quacks and flap their wings high; if pigeons return early to their roost; if the domestic hen tends to stay indoors. And if you prefer the more obscure, how about this one courtesy of Kirkcudbrightshire – "When the crow caws four times it presages rain."

Jackdaws too give warning of bad weather – when they see it coming, they call and flutter around buildings and will often be late flying home at night. The Reverend Swainson, the well-known ornithologist, used to say that marsh harriers would alight in considerable numbers on the Wiltshire Downs before

120

rain – that, of course, was before the Downs were all ploughed up!

When seabirds come far inland it is a sure sign of stormy weather on the coast.

"It must be rough at sea!"

For really foul weather the best-known prophet is the Storm Petrel, otherwise known as Mother Carey's Chicken. The French call them Les Âmes damnées, for sailors believe that they are inhabited by the restless spirits of skippers who ill-treated their crews. We might also add to the list the cock pheasant, who always calls before thunder (it is said that he does the same before supersonic bangs!)

"Old Petrel's being stormy again!"

This is the moment to insert an old Scottish rhyme –

"When ducks are driving through the burn
That night the weather takes a turn."

So, let us take a turn in the weather. Tits, they say, can foresee cold weather. If they stuff themselves with fat or coconut from the bird table, cold weather is imminent. When great tits call, "Ching-Ko, Ching-Ko" there will be a frost within twelve hours. Cock pheasants always call once when they go up to roost; if their calling is prolonged, again, the

122

weather will freeze. This habit is completely reliable, as well as being clearly audible.

"Mum – he's been at the bird table again!"

Now let me offer you a cheerful sign for a change: when the thrush calls loudly at sunset, the morrow will be fine.

One for the cook, and an old one, too –

"In Richmondshire, some persons say that the breastbone of ducks after being cooked are observed to be dark-coloured before a severe winter and much lighter-coloured before a mild winter."

Now for some signs of fine weather on the morrow –

"Swallow high, staying dry; swallow low, wet 't'will blow."

"If the swallows fly high, 'tis a sign of dry." – Both this saying and the last hold true: the swallows are after the midges which fly high in dry weather.

"If the wild geese gang out to sea, good weather there will surely be."

High flying birds, rooks for instance, often foretell fine weather. The general rule is that the farther they fly out and the longer they are in returning, the finer the day. Then there is an old country saying that if a raven is seen in the morning, soaring round and round in circles at a great height and croaking as he does so, it will be a fine day. In the evening, if the bats come out early, tomorrow will be fine. Owls too: if they hoot more than usual, the next day will be fine. Skylarks are particularly noticeable: when they sing for prolonged periods it foretells a fine day.

And for signs of snow: if geese fly due south and high, expect snow very shortly.

To finish, one of the tales of the unexpected: swans flying against the wind means that a hurricane is on the way (I have never confirmed this).

These are just a few of the many signs offered by birds. If those which inhabit your area have not been mentioned here, watch them carefully, and observe what they do when, or just before, it rains. How do they behave before a snowstorm? How do they behave in brilliant sunny weather? Do their singing habits vary? They say, for instance, that the voice of the nightingale sounds harsher before rain. Do other birds' songs alter in the same way? Even superficial observation will soon bring to light a wealth of valuable signals from the bird world. Make careful notes on what you observe. Some blank pages have been deliberately inserted at the end of the book on which to record your own observations. That, after all, is how knowledge is built up.

AN OLD
SAW

Chapter Eight

Old Saws and Earthquakes

So we come to the penultimate chapter of this book. This chapter has been written to include a number of useful observations and sayings which do not fit in exactly in any other part of the book. Some are old saws; a number are obviously culled from seafarers' stores of knowledge; there is a unique gem from China and we end with some information about earthquakes. The latter are not exactly commonplace in England, for which we may be truly thankful, but as these particular signs apply world-wide I have included them here should readers ever find themselves in earthquake country! Forewarned is forearmed.

First, for two confusing old saws – "Mackerel sky, bain't long dry." – Or, if you prefer it – "Mackerel sky, not wet, not dry."

Thence we move into the nautical sphere with –

"Mackerel sky and mares tails, make lofty ships carry low sails."

"Long foretold, long past,
  Short notice, soon past."

"At sea with low and falling glass
Soundly sleeps the careless ass.
Only when it's high and rising
Truly rests the careful wise one."

"When the glass falls low, prepare for a blow:
When it slowly rises high, lofty canvas you may fly."

"When rise begins after low, squalls expect and clear
blow."

Then comes a naval variation on an old friend –

"Evening red and morning grey
Are sure signs of a fine day."
But evening grey and morning red
Makes the sailor shake his head."

And here is another variation on the old theme –

"A red evening and a clear morning sets the pilgrim a-
walking."

The following are some mutually unconnected sayings,
included here because they are all sound words of wisdom!

"A light Christmas, light wheatsheaves."

"A March without water dowers the hind's daughter."

– This sounds obscure, but is actually quite logical: most deer give birth in May, when dry weather is most desirable for the event, so a dry March foretells a dry May. As stated in Chapter Three, a dry March and a rainy April makes a beautiful May.

If you add to that – "East wind in Spring a brilliant summer will bring", and – "When winter meets summer (i.e. no Spring) it foretells a dry, hot summer" – it only goes to show that even in England we may have a fine summer sometimes!

The animal world provides many prognostications of the weather. It is said that when a cat lies with her tail towards the fire, it is a sign of hard weather. When pigs rub themselves in dust, rain is imminent. If moles start working in woodland, and forsake the fields, a drought is imminent – you can add to that the belief that the bigger the molehills are, the milder the winter to come. Water rats, who can anticipate a flood by twelve to eighteen hours, will leave their holes in the river banks and make for higher ground. Next is an old Irish belief: when bees seal their hives, a hard winter lies ahead. Similarly, when wasps "go to bed early" there will be a cold winter. When the white rings on hairy caterpillars are wide, again it will be a hard winter. All these random sayings are true and very reliable.

"We'll start here, Basil"

Moving on to the slightly fantastic, an old countryman I knew believed firmly in the following two sayings –

> "If a hare is seen running down the main street of a town, a bad fire is on the way."

> "If a white hare is seen near a harbour a storm will follow."

Trees can tell us a great deal. Most people know the old one which runs –

> "Oak before ash sign of a splash. Ash before oak sign of a soak."

130

– This is entirely reliable, *provided* that the two are growing close to each other, preferably in the same hedge. Berries are good weather prophets, too. A heavy crop foretells a hard winter, and the earlier the berries appear, the sooner the cold weather will start. The same is true of a heavy crop of acorns. They say of hazel nuts that if they have thick shells it will be a hard winter; if thin, a mild one. Then there is a simple, short saying – "Many haws, many snows." And not forgetting fir cones which open for dry weather and shut up in the wet – this is quite true: they open to shed their seeds which need dry ground for germination. It is also said that if the beech carries a large bud at Christmas, there will be a wet summer.

This one is very old, its origins unsure –

"If thou wilt see and know how it will go that year, then take heed of the oak apples about St Michael's Day. If the apples of the oak trees, when they be cut, be within full of spiders, then followeth a naughty year; if the apples have within them flies, that betokeneth a meetly good year; if there be nothing in them, then followeth a great dearth; if the apples be many and early ripe, so shall it be an early winter, and very much snow shall be before Christmas, and that it shall be cold; if the inner part of the kernel be fair and clear, then shall the summer be fair, and corn good also; if they be lean, then shall there be a hot dry summer; but if they be very moist, then shall the summer be moist also."

– This seems to cover most eventualities. It also seems to obviate the necessity of remembering anything else in this book!

Now a few random reports from different parts of the country –

> "Snow usually falls in the third week in January. If it doesn't fall then it won't fall at all." (Wiltshire)

> "If the March winds start early it will be fine at Easter." (Hampshire)

> "In hot weather, when the wind has been southerly for two or three days, if the clouds are piled like towers one on another, with black on their undersides, there will be sudden thunder and heavy rain." (Somerset)

> "If two such clouds arise, one on either hand, it is time to take shelter hastily." (Gwent)

> "If clouds look dusky, or of a tarnish silver colour, and move very slowly, it is a sign of hail which, if there be a mixture of blue in the clouds, will be small, but if it be very yellow, will be large." (Anon)

Here are a few from the world of water –

> "When a wet season is due, frogs will lay their spawn by the sides of ponds; when a dry season is coming they lay in the middle – in case the pond dries out." –

"When big cod are plentiful in August, expect an early and a hard winter."

"When lobsters end the crawling season early, there will be an early winter."

This leaves only the matter of earthquakes. The only nation which is known to have codified the warning signs is the Chinese; the following extract is taken from Chinese folklore – and it appears to be reliable. "There will be an earthquake soon if –

1.   Horses run wild, kick and rear for no apparent reason.

2.   Chickens will not roost and stay out of doors.

3.   Pigs are unaccountably restless.

4.   Cats carry their kittens out of doors.

5.   Deer leave the forests in droves and shun the woodlands.

6.   Bears (of which we have so many) come out of hibernation.

7.   Snakes leave their nests."

Why, you may ask, should animals behave in these unnatural ways before an earthquake? The theory has been put forward that before a quake an increase of ions in the atmosphere produces an imbalance, to which these animals are sensitive.

A parallel may be drawn with the effect that thunder has on some human beings, who are driven into a state of uncontrollable terror during a thunderstorm.

I would add the following from my own observations, having seen the effect on three occasions. Elongated parallel streamers of cloud, like tightly rolled cotton wool, yellowish-pink in colour, are sometimes seen at sunset. The colour is not unattractive, but is extremely unusual. The phenomenon occurs about the time of an earthquake, which may well be on the other side of the world. The effect is so distinctive as to be quite unmistakable.

To conclude, here is a very long term forecast: Halley's Comet visits the earth every 152 years. In 1531 there was very heavy rain before it came. In 1682 the Thames froze over. In 1834 there were very heavy rains with widespread floods in Europe. 1985 was the wettest summer on record. So watch out in 2137!

Last of all, putting the tongue into the editorial cheek, I give you Uncle Offa's most outrageous statement – "Wednesday is the finest day of the week."

No comment.

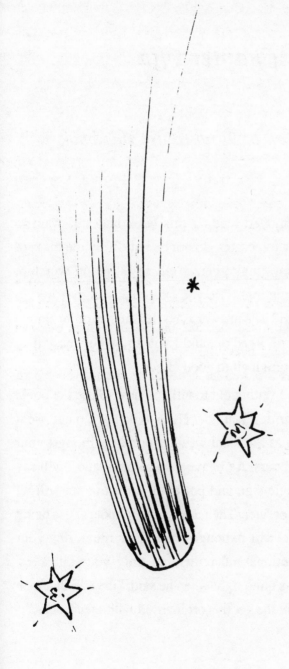

No Comet!

Chapter Nine

Summary, or How to use this book

Dear Reader,

If you have enjoyed reading this book and still want to become a weather forecaster, do not be put off by the mass of fact, fiction, poem, jingle, verse, old saws, moon worship, theories and assumptions. Are you expected, you may ask, to learn it all by heart? The answer is no. It is really quite simple and straightforward. Read on, and I will show how easy it is, and how you can turn it all to good effect.

But first, before setting out to tell you how to use the book, let me start by warning you how NOT to do so. Do not use it to set yourself up as the local weather prophet amongst your friends and neighbours. As I have said before – and I will say again – every single sign and portent known to man will let you down sooner or later. The nature of neighbourliness being what it is, people will expunge from their memories your many sage predictions and remember only your mistakes. Mark Anthony was quite right when he said, "the evil that men do lives after them; the good is oft interred with their bones."

In this picture, can you find nine ways to use this book?

Answers on page 140

So, let your forecasts trickle out casually in conversation and do not trumpet them from the rooftops. It is better to mystify your friends by your reticence than expose your shortcomings by your verbosity.

Accurate reading of the weather requires concentration, observation and persistence. The man who leaves home in the morning, jumps straight into his car, drives to work and shuts himself up in an office all day is unlikely ever to get far as a weather forecaster. It takes time to search out the signs, to note and remember them, and to allot them their relative values. It is not just a question of learning a couple of dozen old saws and spewing them forth both in and out of season.

There is a strict order of precedence in which the various signs and portents should be arranged. First in importance are the Days of Prediction. These are more likely to prove correct than any other signs and they form the foundation of all weather prediction. It is, however, a fact that in some parts of the country some days prove more dependable than others. Why this should be so is more than I can say. Only careful observation will reveal if this is the case in your area. But by and large, the Days of Prediction form a stalwart bed-rock on which to build your forecasts.

Next in importance come the phases of the moon. There are those who would maintain that the moon phases are more dependable than the Days of Prediction, but this, in my experience, is not the case, particularly in the long term. The changes in the weather which occur at the turn of the moon will sometimes conflict with the forecasts of the Days of Prediction: they tend to be more dramatic and sudden than the latter, but as a longer term guide, the Days of Prediction are more likely to be correct. Once the "change day" of the moon phases is established, i.e. the day of or after the turn of the moon on which the weather changes, it will be found to have a surprising regularity and to be very reliable. If you base your forecasts on these two features only, the Days of Prediction and the phases of the moon, the results should not be disappointing.

Third in the scheme of things come the monthly signs. Take particular note of the longer term forecasts which occur in the winter months. These are sufficiently valuable to warrant writing down as they are easily forgotten. Since they are often seventy-five per cent correct, this would be a pity!

The long term forecasts give a sound prediction of the future weather. But the natural signs in the trees and the birds should never be overlooked. They often give clear indications of the weather three or four months ahead. The drawback is that a certain type of tree or species of bird may give a clear signal one year and no signal at all the next. The answer to this is not to rely on one single sign. Observe as many signs as possible and compare them, one against another. It is astounding how many different things will be found to tell the same story. It has long been a theory of mine, as I said in Chapter Seven, that every single species of bird will have something to tell us about the weather at some time of year. If we only know what, when and how . . .

Weather forecasting is an absorbing and abiding hobby, as well as being a useful one. Nobody has yet produced an exhaustive list of all the signs in existence; it would be impossible to do so and new ones are being noted all the time.

Above all, remember that no weather prophet ever gets it one hundred per cent correct. If forecasting were not so difficult and the weather not so changeable there would be no challenge, and the British Character, hardened and honed by its treacherous climate, would not be what it is today.

Your affectionate,
Uncle Offa.

Answers to page 137

1. Doorstop
2. For throwing
3. For reference
4. Mat for hot pots
5. For hiding glasses
6. Dogs toy
7. For broken table legs
8. Several pinches of salt

9. FOR READING

Appendix A

The Forecaster's Year

These are the dates to remember month by month. But it must always be borne in mind that the dates of the new and full moon must also be taken into consideration.

October

18th St Luke

16th to 20th Meteorological Office Quiet period

24th to November 13th, Met Office stormy period

November

1st All Saints' Day

2nd All Souls

11th St Martin

23rd St Clement

25th St Catherine

6th to 13th Buchan's Cold Period

15th to 21st Met Office quiet period

24th to December 14th Met Office stormy period

December	21st St Thomas
	25th Christmas Day
	31st New Year's Eve
	3rd to 14th Buchan's warm period
	25th to 31st Met Office stormy period
	23rd to 31st Pliny's halcyon days

January	1st Janvier Calends
	22nd St Vincent
	25th St Paul
	5th to 17th Met Office stormy period
	18th to 24th Met Office quiet period
	25th to 31st Met Office stormy period

February	2nd Candlemas
	14th St Valentine
	24th St Mattias
	7th to 14th Buchan's cold period
	24th to 28th Met Office stormy period

March	1st St David
	2nd St Chad
	21st St Benedict
	25th Lady Day

April	1st All Fools' Day
	Palm Sunday
	Good Friday
	Easter
	Whitsunday
	11th to 14th Blackthorn Winter, also Buchan's cold period
May	25th St Urban
	9th to 14th Buchan's cold period
June	8th (no saint)
	11th St Barnabas
	15th St Vitus
	24th St John, also Midsummer Day
	Wimbledon Fortnight
	29th to July 4th Buchan's cold period
July	1st (no saint)
	4th to 16th
	15th St Swithun
	12th to 15th Buchan's warm period

August	1st Lammastide
	6th Transfiguration
	24th St Bartholomew
	12th to 15th Buchan's warm period
September	1st (no saint)
	21st Matthew
	29th St Michael
	1st to 17th Met Office quiet period

Appendix B

Dated Predictions

The Meteorological Office

The following dates are reproduced from information supplied by the Meteorological Office, Publications Section, Room 709, London Road, Bracknell, Berks. It is sometimes referred to in the text as "The Met Office"

Quiet Periods

18 – 24 January

1 – 17 September

16 – 20 October

15 – 21 November

The Stormy Periods

5 – 17 January

25 – 31 January

24 – 28 (29) February

24 October to 13 November

24 November to 14 December

25 – 31 December

Alexander Buchan's Predictions

The Cold Periods

7 – 14 February

11 – 14 April

9 – 14 May

29 June to 4 July

6 – 13 November

The Warm Periods

13 – 15 July

12 – 15 August

3 – 14 December

Index

Notes

Notes

Notes

Notes

Notes

Notes

Notes

Notes

Notes